MONKEY ISLAND

Early Praise for *Monkey Island*

❖

"John Morrison's new collection of poems, *Monkey Island*, retains the wry thoughtfulness of his earlier collection *Heaven of the Moment*, and goes further into memory's resonant attention. The sustained sequences such as the title poem and the concluding "Where I Walk" mesmerize with their attention to both ear and soul. These poems commune richly, if sideways, with lost moments, bringing them forward into the always-contemporary heart."

—Ed Skoog, author of *Travelers Leaving for the City*

❖

"*I'll...step into the why and whip of wind, be lifted, left blasted...* so goes *Monkey Island*'s invitation to join poet John Morrison as he faces our long loneliness with poetry's alchemical actions. Morrison initiates transformations in birth, death, God, truth, us, and animals, life and land, water, grit and stink, love and grief, family and blue giraffes— his poems show us what poems can do for us, how they keep what we love close, how they salvage and sanctify our lives."

—Dara Wier, author of *In the Still of the Night*

❖

"How the hell did we become the way we are? Ask John Morrison. He won't tell you, because he doesn't know, but he will provide you exquisite examples with lyrical grace in poems that work like illustrations that accompany certain words in the dictionary. The ghost of God is here, and memory...that strange harbinger reminding us of what we will become. His poems are a little break from the wind, a pause from the chaos, a two-person picnic as we slowly make our way to the grave."

—Carl Adamshick, author of *Birches*

REDBAT
BOOKS
PACIFIC
NORTHWEST
WRITERS
SERIES

Monkey Island

poems by
JOHN C. MORRISON

redbat books
La Grande, Oregon
2020

© 2020 by John C. Morrison

All rights reserved.

Printed in the United States of America

First Edition: December 1, 2020

Trade Paperback ISBN: 978-1-946970-01-5

    Library of Congress Control Number: 2020949141

Published by
redbat books
La Grande, OR 97850
www.redbatbooks.com

Text set in OS Berkeley

Cover painting:
View from Morning by Miró Merrill

Book design by
Kristin Summers, redbat design | www.redbatdesign.com

Table of Contents

My Father the Gorilla — 11

The Family Dog — **13**
    My brothers and I are coming back — 15
    Always in the shadow — 17
    Ghosts terrified me but should one — 18
    In the moonlight the footbridge, a perfect half-arc — 19
    Last fall, on our way — 21
    We've been together all night — 22
    For a full year our dad lived away — 24
    Our plan for the leaves — 26
    My daughter rises a flicker — 27

Your Birth Story — **29**

Sculpture Garden — **35**
    We were away before morning — 37
    To hide I chose — 36
    Late, startled awake, I track — 39
    My mother both moon and sea — 40
    The last wild stretch of Hurricane Creek — 41

One Wind — 43

    Late August the devils — 45
    After the heist — 46
    The world's not a tiny — 48
    The one wind, the odd, runic, lone — 49

Backward Glance — 51

    At the edge of the park town ended — 53
    A mile from the slough, sawgrass — 54
    I hike over a rise — 55
    Dizzy to rip past shirttail — 56
    Trap a rat, searing stink, black — 58

Monkey Island — 59

Where I Walk — 65

    My first house was carved — 67
    The opossum's back glows — 68
    You don't say no — 69
    Buried in the rain, not — 70
    Is your dark ever silky — 71
    By spring my mother — 72

Acknowledgments — 75
About the Author — 77

for Peter Sears

My Father the Gorilla

My own father didn't know
what to do with me. His hairy arms
held me close to hairy chest and I looked up
into his soft, troubled eyes. The church and science
told him you can't have a human child,
but he cared more for me than dogma.

He'd chase my cousins and me
around the yard with a rolling, knuckle-running gait,
whooping and tipping over baby hippos
and stuttering, *You bad monkeys, you bad monkeys,
you bad*. We used pith helmets as bowls
for coconut milk and explorer knives

to scratch our butts and cut ourselves free
from the webs of giant spiders. And for our whole time
together we loved the trees and the breeze at night.
We'd climb into high hammocks we braided
from python skins, sway and hum until we fell asleep.
Then at twenty, I needed more than bananas and grubs,
crouching in the rain with only a leaf for a hat,

and always being wary of poachers and missionaries.
I met my mate on the path by the blue giraffes.
She brought me a pair of trousers and led me away
to have our own children who grow more human
with every tomato. No word in gorilla says forever,
so my father and I slapped each other goodbye.

❖

The Family Dog

My brothers and I are coming back
with a whirly-bird to salvage

all the tractors seized and left
to rust in the wheat. The tractors

that muscled the farmer one more
furrow and no farther. Sure,

he unbuckled the hood and checked
for spark, primed the tinny

carburetor again and again,
cursed and walked for a wrench across

the turned dirt, gave up on
the goddamn in thin moonlight. We're

coming back for the machinery
out to pasture and melting down

scrap to pour a new spine for our
national Renaissance. We have

to wear ear plugs and hard hats.
One brother will pilot,

hold the giant copter steady
against gusty winds as the other two

rappel down bulky chains, secure
the hulk, a dot in the heartland,

Monkey Island | 15

with heavy hooks and whisk our prize
away across the sky to the giant caldron

smoky red as a demon eye. We move west
after Midwest, haul off junker cars

tipped in arroyos, flimsy
forgotten mobile homes that stink

of ammonia and mold, all dropped into
the molten roil, then the giant

odd jacks of failed public art,
then the giant, burnished, silly, silver "O's."

❖

Always in the shadow
the north side of the mountain
our town of scrap

wood and old tin,
duct tape and tarpaper
never had a name.

Never claimed, christened,
never chartered we remained
incorporeal as wind

that gusted with sand grains.
In the boonies we bruised
where the Bogeyman watched

us sleep. We refused Welcome,
Pistachio, Harbinger, Zeal.
Our Post Office a bucket,

a boulder our idiot, we
called where we collected
the dry and cold

forgotten in scrub oaks
between prairie and scabland,
scabland and gravelly arroyo.

We lotioned our elbows
and whispered day to day
in a dialect of moth.

❖

Ghosts terrified me but should one
take a swipe with fist
or bloody chain, the ethereal blow
would just swish through my face. But the Devil,

Lucifer himself, roasted to a dark crimson
in the fires, his two horns like thorns
of a huge rose, he frightened me down
to my groin. I hated everyone completely.
Sins stained me, stuck to my fingers and palms

like pine pitch. There were not enough decades
of Joyful or Sorrowful Mysteries to see
me clear of damnation, an eternal
pressure cooker not for rattling jars
of sweet summer peaches but for my bones

and those of the equally luckless dead
locked forever in a roil of flame. To banish
the Devil, one must banish God, too,
a *quid pro quo* that began my long loneliness outside

the company of angels and saints. The day
I held open the secret backdoor of my soul
and said, *you two must go,* silent, they stood
up from their tea in the kitchen nook
and walked past me like two severe

yet frail uncles, each with a hitch
in the step, both disgusted and shamed,
back into the pagan forest, one a whiff
of mushroom, one a brush of morning breeze.

❖

In the moonlight the footbridge, a perfect half-arc,
looks carved of ivory. My son and I
cross to a path lit by little stone pagodas.
Beneath the ginkgos, we hunch with walking sticks
like wise men and travel to the power plant
beside the ocean to praise the Samurai
who go inside to stanch great gouts of poison steam.
When they return at night, weak, you can see
their sick livers in their yellow eyes. We help them

undress and rinse, and then lotion their burns.
I'm here to stop my son
from stepping into a containment suit
and sacrificing his life. I'm here to say
the one to go, if anyone goes, is me. I'm strong.
I understand valves and wrenches, pressure
and the idiom of isotopes, and I know my obligation
to country and air and the sea.
The disease, opaque as curdles in the vein,
will have less time to work in me. When the Samurai rise,

we hold the arms of their gowns for them,
hold the rubber boots for skinny feet.
They lick their thumbs, anoint our foreheads,
and we pray for the Samurai.
In time, all of them will die of an explosion
or the turn of their blood. We collect
and smoke their cigarettes for them with dedication

as we stand in view of the generator
while they strive inside, the radiation a prickle
on our skin. We listen for a buried thunder,

the walls of the plant giving way like the soft bones
of a sea monster rolled onto the beach to rot.

for Jackson

Last fall, on our way
to a funeral, my sister Annette
and I traveled in her little blue car

on backroads through the small towns
that harvest wind off the delta
with an army of splay-handed
giants. The morning was calm and we
tooled through before the windmills woke

to sweep their arms to spin a single amp.
The eucalyptus, which must the air
with portents, hadn't so much
as twitched their long, grey leaves.
The houses, Victorian farmhouses,

slept in silent as a grudge.
In the stillness, we felt the somber pull
of the service ahead. I needed
a new sight, a long crisp track
into the mountains and a railroad

to run like a model train past
the giants' feet with a cheery clickity-clack
and passengers with bright faces
to wave from the windows
and assure me my time had yet to come.

❖

We've been together all night. On
the ferry, God, in black, acts the ass,
embarrasses himself, brags He can end us,
all sapiens in an instant,
all sparrows, too. He wouldn't dare

dish this shit if the Holy Spirit
were here to twist His ear, so Mike
in a glorious bravado
reaches over, gives God enough of a shove
He trips, topples right into the sound.

The splash kicks up as the ferry powers past.
We know we're in for it. We also know
no real harm done to someone named
Almighty. He'll be furious,
we'll take our lumps, hope He's outgrown
his Old Testament temper. Off the ferry,

Mike and I park downtown, sit
in the back of the pickup then wait for God
when out of a side alley He runs, through traffic,
right at us. In an embrace of the inevitable
while simply clowning we wave,
yell, "Hey, God, over here."

He's soaked, pissed. Never has a moment
been more precious. We climb down out of the truck,
hug Him, say sorry, ask if he's OK.
Though He's mad enough to teach us a profound
lesson in the Chain of Being, He's charmed
by our high-spirits and hijinks.

And we are contrite. Pushing anyone
off a moving ferry is wrong,
regardless of how omniscient He might be.
We bow, eyes closed so He can talk to us
inside our heads, then I pull the ratty
army blanket from behind the seat,

help God from his sopping shirt, pants,
lace boxers, socks like sea slime, down to the flesh
none of us can see and say the same way. I see mirror.
What the dark moon sees. Myself
in negative. I see a passage and down the passage
a child on the other side of the world,
her bright face the size of a quarter. I look
to His sad, waterlogged feet, wrinkled old

as though pickled then we wrap Him snug
and all sit in the back of the pick-up
in the warm peach of a morning sun,
smoke cigarettes, drink coffee, sing
slow and deep, *Swing Low Sweet Chariot*.

For a full year our dad lived away
on an island and flew planes
heavy with missiles and gold
and on weekends would golf
with gorillas. At home, our mother

was lost in the pantry or the laundry,
the attic or behind the waterheater
where she'd opened the electrical panel
and with trouble light and butter knife

tinkered with the base circuitry
of our home. Summer, my older brothers
found a shaded bank along Wild Horse Creek,
where they and their sixteen-year-old friends
could drink beer and slug each other.

My oldest sister neglected her hair
and washed the dishes. My next sister
read historical novels in her room
for nine straight days, slept for three,
and went back to reading. My little sister

sucked a pebble and kept asking,
where's Dad? I'd say, *Sis, the plane,
the missiles, the gold, the golf, the gorillas,
remember?* Then the lights would flicker out
and from deep in the house we'd hear
mother curse, *damn*. They'd flicker

back on and the big fan in the living room,
a monster my size by the name of *Arctic Breeze*,
with a blade like my father's propeller,
would wind up to a deep, resonant whirr
and spit a subtle rose-water from a reservoir

our mother filled each morning with a potion
of crushed red and yellow velvet petals.
I was the family dog, sniffing the trail
by the creek, sniffing the steps
to the basement, the threshold of my sister's room,
the clean plates in the dish drainer, the family dog,

unless I was a boy answering my sister
gold, golf, remember? Missiles, gorillas?
Or lying on the living room floor,

damp in fragrance, or wrenching
the rabbit ears right on the TV
to scare away the ghost stalking
Daniel Boone and his Cherokee blood-brother,
the fey yet lethal Mingo,
a TV I would now and then hug.

Our plan for the leaves
is to burn them all
and all at once in a mountain heap
the night before the rains roll in
and rot their crisp color to slop.

A conflagration, yes, worthy
of the end. Birch, sweetgum, willow,
the flouncy scraps of fall,
oak, elm, ginkgo.
One big fire.
Huge. In fact, bon.
I'll recruit my fireman uncles
Hector and Jess
back from the dead and glad
to be the chiefs

who hand out the same sturdy toy firehats
they gave us as kids.
We'll skip around
hollering in the flickering light
of the bonfire as they
stand back and cross their arms
and see we keep the high sparks
from catching aflame
the flickering nuggets of ice
we call stars.

My daughter rises a flicker
of sunlight, rises like the eerie
yellow glow of autumn
maple leaves, like the shadow
of a tree trunk at dusk. She rises

like a rune. Like a song sparrow,
like the long hush of a slow
tide. She never was. She
never held my hand.
Never will. Will never

call from a distance. Walk
the deer path beside the creek. Start
a new story beginning with ferns.
End without her light

laughter like the chime
of crystal inside the open
front door. Stones are more
alive. A lie more alive.

Your Birth Story

You were born underwater. You were
born on a train at night. Born
as the sun rose over the bed
of the old pickup, set over
a mint field, and rose again
across the Atlantic.

*

Your father was bowling. He was on
a plane. Your father farmed apricots
in Kansas. Your father,
who is your father? Your father
breathed for your mother. He rode
her contractions like waves. How odd
to say like waves, with you born beneath
the crest like a seal. Your gooey fist
held the last bit of the first dark.

*

The trees had blossomed, blossomed and lost
their leaves and stood in the morning
sunlight. You know the weather: you brought
the wind with you. The weather was calm,
clear and cold and fair. We wore
shorts and sweaters and silk. You wore
a hat, knit, like a watch cap. You
were born in the trees under a wave
because you were with your father.

*

The same day apples fell. Same day
snow fell. Same day people crowded
the square. They gave you
astronomy, one constellation at a time.
You gave them braids. You gave them
bracelets and molasses. The same day
salmon gave up on us. Same day
rains arrived so soft we never noticed.

*

You were named after a robot, the robot
friend of a robot, after your great-
grandfather, for a friend, for a fish,
for a first baseman, for a cloud,
for a moment, for your mother, for
a stone, for the slant of light, for
the bend of light underwater, for good luck.
You were named by witches. You
were named for the click of your mind.

*

Your brother was missing. Your brother
was behind you. Your sister was missing.
Your sister was inside you. Your brother
waited on the bank. Your grandmother
held him and her and all
who would come. Your children held you.
The first one held you. The first one
held you and cried.

*

In your hand you held a token
for the T. A key to the cylindrical
season. A tether. A bead. A
secret. And another. You came holding
a gift for the departed, for the quick,
for passage, for promise, for balm.
Your eyes were open. One
was open. One was blue the other
midnight. Your eyes were open to see
what you'd left inside, beneath, under-
water, and your digits were webbed
and your head was shaped like a fez
and you, the witches told us, were perfect.

Sculpture Garden

We were away before morning,
before birdsong. We were coffee
and quiet voice, a bite
of apple. We were three

brothers and I mean by blood
and nothing sentimental,
three by chance born
to Margaret and John
with shotguns in the thin
leaf-laced light and long
shadows of an almond orchard,

our boots on the cool, turned soil
waiting for the flock we knew
would pass over on the flight
to dawn water. Three
who watched and whispered
about girls' hair, arrowheads,
a shed rattler's skin, and listened

for wings and when a single
dove flew above us and we
in three blasts scattered shot
along the bird's line, the flutter
fell over the stand of willow
to the irrigation ditch. Then

I, the youngest, sent to paddle
after the kill, slid naked, goose-fleshed
into the sting of bright water.

❖

To hide I chose
the old oak
the many airy rooms

among burly limbs
not ghost-invisible
or gone but away

aloft and alone
held by a giant who swayed
tiny between breaths

❖

Late, startled awake, I track
his steps across the star chart
embedded in my dream ceiling.
He pauses at window, slips
down the stairs. The screen door
groans like my boyhood back
gate. He's out to see what burns
the night with phosphorus, what
turns the oak, fence, neighbor's chimney
to marble.
   I trail him and together
in boxers, in the pale light
and passing gravity of the cold
round rock that arcs over
and around us, we look up, brothers
exhumed from sleep, two statues set
in the moon's sculpture garden.

for Will

My mother both moon and sea
smoked and sipped her pink summer gin
while I the plump pollywog
swayed all grotesque grin and eye
out and in on her tides
flexed my translucent spine
long knobby tail
niblet toes

The last wild stretch of Hurricane Creek
runs back behind the barn
where my uncle and I, gloved
and muddy, grip, brace and yank out
briar by roots for pasture. I am
proud and grateful he has chosen me

for labor and conversation. Unlike my father
he isn't afraid I'll gash myself
with the sickle or stumble
and stab him backside. I know all
I think doesn't matter in the world
but I hum along anyway between grunts,

my muscles flush and steady,
as my mind defies the chore
and starts upstream to meet you
on the trail down in the grey and heavy
humidity that means brief showers
of big drops to chase other hikers
away from the pool tucked at a turn
in the hills. We strip and slip pale into

the cool green water we share
with a pair of floating turtles,
and find each other for a long kiss.

❖

One Wind

Late August the devils
scuff across plowed fields
empty except for dust,
a dozen dusky pillars
waver toward dry,
white sky. They whirl

to the river, faint in a gold
sheen. One day as I itch
and sweat no car behind
no farm town tucked
beneath a canopy
of cottonwoods, I'll raise
arms and step into

the why and whip of wind,
be lifted, left blasted
spitting a gritty tongue.

After the heist
we can drop by the gloomy
little bakery, step into the soft
aromas and pick up a dozen
macaroons, pink. Sit on a stone bench
outside the museum
of Natural History, count

our loot into the high
three-hundreds, and I can ask
how you feel whenever you see
the skeleton of a wooly mammoth,
the bones tea-stained to a shiny,
rich mahogany. Puzzled? Amused?
Empty? A wooly mammoth

with a big boney dome crammed
with all her smarts and kindness
could be a first-rate friend once we
run her through the car wash a few
times. *Close your eyes, Little Sister! Close
your eyes!* We'd never be cold
at night, the whole

family wound in the deep pile
of her pelt, asleep in
the oceanic swells of her
husky breathing and dreaming
austere tundra dreams. Gentle
with any talk of extinction.

No one takes the topic well.
When we can't keep enough cereal
in the house, can't make nearly enough
popcorn balls for snacks, we'll lead her
by trunk to the breadth

of the Zumwalt prairie, the vast
grassland, into quiet
contemplation and sere winds.
She'd browse and amble and fit in
out there, eyed from the distance
by wolves, just like at home
in prehistory.

The world's not a tiny
toybox: there's room aplenty
for a plastic sack of grit, corners

for just a pinch, dozens
of drainpipes for a dash. The debris
can be so difficult, bits of skull,
femur, the knot of a gold cap.
An old sock is a weak idea. The ocean
always works, oysters to mother
another harvest of pearls, warmed

every once long while around
a lover's neck. Sprinkled on lava
is a cute trick, become a crust
of earth. Sucked in an industrial
vacuum is just a stall. Fired
for a water glass and the lip collects
missed kisses. Out of a cannon

over a canyon, blown off with a big
bellows, poured in cement for sidewalk
chalk or a dam to hold a river
back. Laced in a commercial batch

of potpourri, finally smell sweet.
Soothe. The next of kin could tender
a plan. Drive the remains to some
lame marsh. Ash, impossible to end.

The one wind, the odd, runic, lone
wind, that discrete, big buffet
is the one I can't understand.
I understand gusts, fickle and shifty.
Gust. Wait. Gust. Wait. Wait. Gust.

Another may be along, who knows.
Pages riffle. Caps fly. Gusts say
the season is pouty, fussy
enough every few minutes to make
trouble. And breezes. Breezes make
perfect sense as a long line of ghost children

of different heights who chase
across an afternoon. Still, the one
wind eludes me. Blusters through
like a drunk angel who slaps down

spider webs, tugs laundry off the line,
slams doors left ajar. And I even
understand whole days of wind
intent on racket, on hectoring trees
and arranging then rearranging
the fallen leaves, days of wind

that snap the faded flag and whip
away the neighborly hello.
I grew up with such hooligans,
who in late summer would leave
the ocean straits to carouse. The one

wind, though, brusque passerby;
I don't get the anger. I don't understand
the enmity toward stillness or
the problem with the lamp at the window.

Backward Glance

At the edge of the park town ended
in a ditch and across the ditch

hobos camped in the wild grass
moved like shadows at dusk.

Whenever our turn came to chase
the ball down into the reeds

and stink, the still water black,
we were afraid of leeches

already on our hands and calves
each a living bruised welt

like a bite in a nasty fight
and we were warned how a bum

could grab you, shove a filthy
rag in your mouth, break your elbow

backward, make you beg in the cold
of a city far off for quarters he'd use

for booze and be the father
so your father could never find you.

❖

A mile from the slough, sawgrass
and gulls, the chimp squatted in the bare
yard, chained to iron post. He never
more than whimpered as I waved

goodbye and hated whoever lived in the cold
ranch house, filled his water bucket,
then left for the day. He couldn't help
the stink of crap scattered around
his circled range, caked in his sparse,
wiry hair. No pond to wade in or wash,

no oak to curl beneath to nap. He had
the grey lips of my grandfather asleep
in his beige chair, though now I'm afraid
my grandmother, collared, draws a finger

in dust. Never a circus prankster, what
would he be, happy? Kidnap out
of the question, jungle impossible,
King of Monkey Island at the zoo
still the zoo, instead the worse
sentence. Shit his only toy, I could've
brought him an umbrella for the afternoon

high clouds would bolster and rain, a metal
puzzle of three looped rods, a pickle. I knelt.
Spoke softly into his gooey, broken
eyes. Held his rough, filthy hand.

I hike over a rise
into a cattle herd
that thinks I'm a ranch hand
bringing a salt block.

The burden of their bulk limps
toward me like the dead
with tongues filthy as oven mitts
moist eyes crowded with flies.

Dizzy to rip past shirttail
and panties
I lay down on my back

on rough clods in the old
furrow left fallow
scraggly spring grass

now golden around us I was
as underground
as I have ever been halfway

in shallow grave a plow-depth
closer to corpse
and I whimpered to hurry

hurry before a boy out hunting
quail might kick
across the dry field onto us

in our scuff and hum a little
bit of sky
over her new shoulder outside

the curtain of hair she sorry
for my back
bare ass I for the grit

and the grind on her pale
knees the wear
on us enough we finish without

any sweet linger a tangle without
a moment's hush
to hear the crows dusted we rose

Trap a rat, searing stink, black
eyes, whiskers, soft ears,
pinned by her snaky tail alive

wondering where's my mother
whose neck's snapped in another corner,
you know you will be a killer.

Let go, she'll return to the rafters
in the garage or worse, stray
across the grape arbor and gnaw
into the crawl space and you'll hear
her skitter as she nests for a mischief

of pups deep in cottony insulation
like a cloud in the dark or a vision
of heaven at night. Cured of the fatal

allure of bacon, wise to the scent
of guile, she and forever her progeny
will never be fooled by another
trap. The commotion above your insomnia

will blur into the single voice, weak
and hoarse, a dying man whose one wish
is to drink from a fountain dedicated

with a plaque *To All Good That Was*
with sparkly water that sips sweet
as a last backward glance.

Monkey Island

Cleaning up junk
left over from making
the universe, the first monkey
dropped a meteor,
seared all the surrounding trees

now the monkeys
press their hand and footprints
into the still-steaming metal
to mark their moment
in the creamy gleam.

    *

Monkeys always argue
their favorite color,

mid-day, the sky just above
the boulder. The translucent ear
of a newborn. What dolphins
breathe. Inside an oyster shell.

The cave mouth. Lava
at night. Fresh coconut meat. Palm
of the great mother after
she rubs her chin. Her chin.

*

For the winter solstice,
the monkeys trail long strands
of tinsel for one more night.

They ache the next day
and sleep on the beach.

The children bury them
in the sand up to
their faces and the faces
become a long path
of stepping stones.

*

To escape the thieves
who come one night

all monkeys
climb down and hide
inside coconuts
for sixty-one years.

*

When a storm
rolled a giant spot light
up out of the lagoon
half the monkeys
want to gut the metal
for decorations and turn
the large drum into a toy.

They keep the spotlight whole
for their plays. Always a scuffle
and monkeys bite
to be on the stage crew:
Spotlight the villain!
Spotlight the couple kissing
in the wings! Spotlight
the magic stone in the hand!
Stay with the stone!

    *

In the red typhoon
even old monkeys
are scared when flying fish
pelt the island.

The typhoon left behind
golden glass floats in the lagoon
a cave open where there was no cave.
and a deflated silk balloon
draped the trees like the slinky
negligee of a giantess.

    *

One sunset, every
monkey took a turn
inside the pillar of flame
and every monkey
ached to share the light
with loved monkeys

no longer alive.
Each thought
I want to hug
the missing monkey
who already gave
their body to the river.

Where I Walk

My first house was carved
into a wall of wind. The world
was wind. Inside we

were wind, the whoosh
of blood the whoosh
of red wind, regular and

unforeseen. Our nerves
belonged to the wind. You hid
like a mole in a tunnel

or stubborn stayed
to roughen in the wind.
At night we slept in

the wind and the scent
now of distant animals, now
a forest to the north,

and now the ocean stings
our lips. The wind flowed
like light through the fingers
of a god who didn't

always believe in kindness.
Touched our ears,
slapped with an open hand.

The opossum's back glows
like a rough sack of full moon

as I plant peas she rustles
out of honeysuckle, sees me, seizes,

then retreats into umber and leaves
an emissary from sleep, quiet

as a breeze through a screen door,
with a waddle and an ease

as though the succulent slugs
she hunts are laced with laudanum.

You don't say no
like a screen door
slammed but

no no no
like the door unlatched
eased out and back
by a night wind

Buried in the rain, not
in a rainstorm, not in the middle

of a rainfall, in the rain,
a warm rain in a winter,

we buried him in the rain
like you would return a child

to a mother's womb. We buried
him in the rain when he

was already the dew point of lichen.
We split open the clear rain,

slipped him inside, and waved
goodbye. We buried him

in the rain and touched the rain.

❖

Is your dark ever silky
as old port or soft as the underside
of a calendula petal with your eyes
closed, or is your dark more like a knobby

patch of summer tar mounded in
a pothole, the same tar the dumb
kid would twist off in a wad
to chew like *Black Jack* gum?
Without any of the warm light
in that memory, just the oily,

shiny, black and sticky, a syrup
in ears and eyes, down your throat
and nose, until you're full
or swallowed, or is your dark
my dark, a black gravel

with a few, flickering grey
pebbles sifted in, all in
motion like a slow storm, a fine
emery cloth on the skin, a grim
spa, yes, brisk, but no doubt
grinding me down.

for Peter Sears

By spring my mother
will be the size of a gnome
and could become lost
as the garden leafs out.

Mother, I'll call,
Mother, would you like some tea?

A rustle in the hydrangea
where she's made a little nest
to stay cool come summer

and she peeks out.
Cinnamon?

Yes, mother,
I say,
Cinnamon, in your blue mug,

cobalt blue from a doll's china set.
I cup her up onto my shoulder
and we stroll to the kitchen nook

as she chatters about the wind chime
and how sweet
the neighbor's one-eyed cat.
I tell her soon

she will be too tiny
to be out by herself
because of the nasty
scrub jay and before I
too begin to shrink

I can make a room for her
in an acorn charm
around my neck

until she is so wee
she fits among the molecules
where I walk and breathe

walk and breathe.

Acknowledgments

My sincere appreciation goes to the editors at these publications in which the following poems first appeared under the following titles:

Aperçus Quarterly: "Dove"
Basalt: "The Next Glory Be"
Beloit Poetry Journal: "Furrow"
Cider Press Review: "Our Plan for the Leaves"
Cloudbank: "Sculpture Garden"
Cobalt Review: "Cattle"
The Comstock Review: "My Daughter" and "We Were Warned"
The Cortland Review: "The Last Wild Stretch of Hurricane Creek"
Fourteen Hills: "Japanese Footbridge"
Hubbub: "Your Birth Story"
The Midwest Quarterly: "Inside the Rain"
Phantom Drift: "Opossum," and "The Uncles"
Poetry Northwest: "Where I Walk"
Red Rock Review: "One Wind"
RHINO: "Pollywog"
Slant: "We Start with Tractors"
Spillway: "You Don't Say No"
Spoon River Poetry Review: "The Last Step of the Plan"
Windfall: "Wind"

"The Uncles" appeared in *Alive at the Center*, published by Ooligan Press.

My deep and ongoing gratitude to fellowship that helped shape these poems and this book. To my generous writing community: the Odds, the SOPS, the devout at Po' Church, and the Attic Institute. Deep appreciation to Dave Jarecki and Sara Guest for their creative conflict resolution and to the other readers along the way who went into the weeds to kick this can back onto the path: Kirsten Rian, Matt Schumacher, Willa Schneberg, Carl Adamshick, Ed Skoog, Jeff Alessandrelli, and David Memmott.

Great thanks to Kristin Summers and Greg Johnson at redbat books for believing in the work, doing the work, and giving my work a home.

The lessons my teachers Tom Rabbitt, Debora Greger, Pat Carter passed down still encourage. Gary Thompson and Dara Wier always know their way with warm, wise, kind word. Peter Sears, generous with a *bravo*, was never shy to share from his grand storehouse.

I'm also so lucky that Miró Merrill found her way to Monkey Island and brought back the canvas. My love to my mother, my father who leads the entire Munkum clan, my brothers and sisters, my boys, and to my partner of so many loving travels, Kim Anne Thomas. She makes poetry possible.

About the Author

John C. Morrison lives in Portland, Oregon. His first book, *Heaven of the Moment*, won the Rhea & Seymour Gorsline poetry competition and was a finalist for the Oregon Book Award in Poetry. He teaches for Portland Community College and at the Attic Institute as an Associate Fellow. He is also an associate editor for the fabulist journal of literature, *Phantom Drift*.

For other titles available from redbat books, please visit:
www.redbatbooks.com

Also available through Ingram, Bookshop.org,
Amazon.com, Powells.com and by special order through
your local bookstore.

www.ingramcontent.com/pod-product-compliance
Lightning Source LLC
Chambersburg PA
CBHW020958090426
42736CB00010B/1371